34880000 823240

BOOK CHARGING CARD

976.2
WIN

Accession No. _____ Call No. WIN

Author Winans, Jay D.

Title IOWA | Date

976.2
WIN

Winans, Jay D.
IOWA

34880000823240

IOWA

Jay D. Winans

Published by Weigl Publishers Inc.
123 South Broad Street, Box 227
Mankato, MN 56002
USA
Web site: http://www.weigl.com

Library of Congress Cataloging-in-Publication Data

Winans, Jay D.
    Iowa / Jay D. Winans.
        p. cm. -- (A kid's guide to American states)
    Includes bibliographical references and index.
    ISBN 1-930954-38-7
    1. Iowa--Juvenile literature. [1. Iowa.] I. Title. II. Series.

F621.3 .W56 2001

2001017999

    ISBN 1-930954-81-6 (pbk.)

Printed in the United States of America
1 2 3 4 5 6 7 8 9 10   05 04 03 02 01

Project Coordinator
Michael Lowry
Substantive Editor
Rennay Craats
Copy Editor
Bryan Pezzi
Designers
Warren Clark
Terry Paulhus
Layout
Susan Kenyon
Photo Researcher
Diana Marshall

Photograph Credits

CONTENTS

Introduction 4

Land and Climate 8

Natural Resources 9

Plants and Animals 10

Tourism 12

Industry 13

Goods and Services 14

First Nations 16

Explorers and Missionaries 17

Early Settlers 18

Population 20

Politics and Government 21

Cultural Groups 22

Arts and Entertainment 24

Sports 26

Brain Teasers 28

For More Information 30

Glossary 31

Index 32

Iowa is one of the wealthiest agricultural states in the country. More than 90 percent of the state's land is farmable.

INTRODUCTION

A major farming state, Iowa plays an important role as one of the nation's main breadbaskets. Vast cornfields and massive hog farms have supplied the country with food for several decades. Iowa is often described as "one giant farm" that does everything from harvesting crops to packaging foods. Iowa's rolling prairie farmland stretches from the Mississippi River to the Missouri River. Its rich earth produces some of the most abundant crops in the world. Located in the midwestern United States, Iowa lies between the flat prairie states to the west and the forested industrial states to the east.

QUICK FACTS

Iowa is a Native-American word meaning "this is the place" or "the beautiful land." The state was named after the Iowa River, which was named after the Iowa peoples.

Iowa entered the Union on December 28, 1846, as the twenty-ninth state.

Iowa's state bird is the eastern goldfinch.

Iowa has the third-largest number of farms in the country. There are approximately 95,000 farms within the state.

The Des Moines International Airport employs more than 3,800 people.

Getting There

Iowa shares its borders with Minnesota to the north, Wisconsin and Illinois to the east, Missouri to the south, and Nebraska and South Dakota to the west.

Getting to Iowa is simple thanks to the state's many roadways and airports. The state's **rural** road system connects Iowa's sparse population, which is spread over 56,275 square miles. With more than 112,700 miles of highway, Iowa's farmers never have trouble sending their goods to markets or to shipping stations. Iowans and visitors also use these roads to explore the state by car. For those who prefer air travel, Iowa has more than 300 airports and airfields. Most of the state's major cities enjoy air service, but Iowa's busiest airport is the Des Moines International Airport. Much of the state's commercial traffic is shipped by barge along the Missouri and Mississippi Rivers.

QUICK FACTS

The state flag has three vertical stripes—red, white, and blue. The central white stripe contains a bald eagle carrying a blue streamer with the state's motto.

IOWA

The state motto is "Our Liberties We Prize and Our Rights We Will Maintain."

Although Iowa has been a state since 1846, its present boundaries were not drawn until 1857.

The Great Seal of Iowa pictures a soldier standing in a wheat field in front of the Mississippi River. Above the soldier, an eagle carries the state motto.

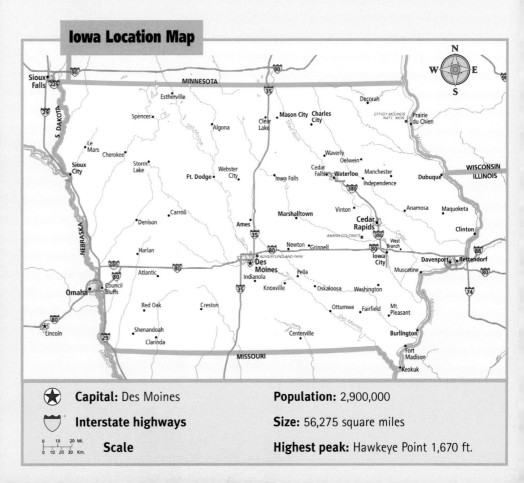

Iowa Location Map

Capital: Des Moines

Interstate highways

Scale
0 10 20 Mi.
0 10 20 30 Km.

Population: 2,900,000

Size: 56,275 square miles

Highest peak: Hawkeye Point 1,670 ft.

The stainless steel 60-foot-tall Tree of Five Seasons stands at the site of the first log cabin that was built in Cedar Rapids.

Native Americans were Iowa's first inhabitants. It was not until the late-seventeenth century that French explorers arrived in the area. Like most of the states along the Mississippi River and throughout the Midwest, the first Europeans to settle Iowa were adventurous people from the eastern states and Europe. These early settlers had set out westward in search of money and freedom.

Settlers often took over Native-American land by force and claimed it for themselves. Many conflicts were fought between Native Americans and settlers, as well as among the Native Peoples themselves. In 1832, Iowa was the site of the Bad Axe Massacre. The massacre claimed the lives of many Sauk and Meskwaki, who were killed by the United States Army while crossing the Mississippi River into Iowa. Bad Axe was the final defeat for the Sauk and Meskwaki in what became known as the **Black Hawk War**.

Iowa's quiet rural charm is evident in its many small towns. Nestled into the Mississippi River valley, Lansing has a modest population of 1,050 people.

QUICK FACTS

Iowa is known as "The Hawkeye State," a tribute to Black Hawk, leader of the Meskwaki and Sauk in the early 1800s.

The state tree is the oak. It is a common tree found throughout Iowa.

Throughout its history, Iowa has remained a collection of small towns and farms. No major cities were ever built. To this day, Iowa's cities remain fairly small.

The United States acquired Iowa from France as part of the **Louisiana Purchase** in 1803.

In 1993, Iowa suffered through the most devastating flood in the history of the United States. Over 23 million acres of land in the upper Midwest were covered by water. After the flood, it was discovered that the waters had uncovered an ancient ocean floor. More than 250,000 visitors from around the United States flocked to the area to walk on the 375-million-year-old bedrock and search for fossils in the limestone.

In 1993, intense rainstorms led to severe flood damage in all ninety-nine of Iowa's counties.

At its heart, Iowa remains a very large collection of rural communities. One of the most important **grass roots** political movements started in Iowa. In 1854, the Republican Party began because a few Iowans, and others from neighboring states, shared a vision of what the country should be. They held small meetings in their homes to discuss that vision. Various artistic and literary movements also have their origins in Iowa.

QUICK FACTS

The 1839 dispute between Iowa and Missouri over Iowa's southern border is known as the Honey War. The two states almost came to blows over three bee trees along the border. The situation was resolved before any actual fighting occurred.

Clark's Tower, in Madison County, pays tribute to Iowa's pioneer past. Built in 1926, it is a 25-foot-tall memorial to one of the county's first pioneer families.

Oktoberfest celebrations are held at the Amana Colonies every year during the first weekend of October. This German-style festival includes traditional music and dance, arts, crafts, food, and a parade.

The lowest temperature ever recorded in Iowa was –47°F, in Elkader on February 3, 1996.

LAND AND CLIMATE

Iowa has a prairie landscape of rolling hills and sloping valleys. It is part of the region called the Central Lowlands, which consists of plains, hills, and excellent farmland. Iowa's soil in the northcentral region is especially rich. Despite Iowa's generally flat landscape, parts of the state contain ridges, cliffs, and steep valleys. A **watershed** runs from the state's northwestern corner to its southeastern corner. Many streams and rivers crisscross the state, but the Mississippi and Missouri Rivers are by far the largest in Iowa. The Missouri River runs along the western edge of the state, while the Mississippi River makes up the eastern border.

Iowa's climate is extreme, with temperatures ranging from as low as –30° Fahrenheit in the winter to as high as 108°F in the summer. January temperatures average 14°F in the northwest and 22°F in the southeast. Summer temperatures range from 72°F in the north to 76°F in the south.

The Loess Hills are named for the fine-grained loess, or clay, which was deposited there after the last Ice Age.

Soil of the quality found in Iowa is very rare in the world. Iowa is said to have one-fifth of the world's Grade A soil.

NATURAL RESOURCES

Iowa's most important natural resource is its dark, rich soil. Continental ice sheets covered the area during different ice ages from 10,000 to 1.6 million years ago. Each time the ice retreated, it left deposits of glacial silt, which are the basis for the high-quality soils.

At one time, Iowa's soils were even more fertile than they are today. Over the years, overuse of the soil led to a decrease in productivity. Today, proper farm management, and development and use of **hybrid** crop species has once again increased productivity.

Iowa is taking steps to harness its **renewable** resources, such as wind and solar energy. By 2015, the state plans to have 10 percent of its energy produced by alternative energy resources.

QUICK FACTS

Iowa is the third-largest producer of wind-generated electricity in the United States.

Minerals produced in Iowa include **gypsum**, lime, and coal.

The state rock of Iowa is the geode. Iowa is known around the world for its high numbers of these beautiful and rare rock formations. The inside of the geode is covered in crystals.

There are more than 300 wind turbines in Iowa.

PLANTS AND ANIMALS

Many of the grasses and flowers that once covered Iowa's prairies were cleared to make way for new farmland. Some prairie flowers can still be found in ditches and roadsides across the state. Iowa has many other beautiful wildflowers, including pasqueflowers, asters, phloxes, lilies, and wild indigo brooms. The state flower, the wild prairie rose, grows throughout the state.

A large proportion of Iowa's forests have been cut down, but almost 1.5 million acres remain. The eastern red cedar is the only evergreen tree that is native to every county in Iowa. While it no longer thrives in the same numbers as it once did along the Cedar River, it can still be found in the **windbreaks** of farms across the prairie.

The chestnut oak, also called the chinquapin oak, is named after its leaves, which resemble chestnuts.

QUICK FACTS

Trees common to Iowa include hickory, maple, elm, pine oak, and chestnut oak. Twelve different species of oak are native to the state of Iowa.

Tall, thick fields of prairie grasses once covered 80 percent of Iowa. Since then, more than 90 percent of the state has been transformed into farmland.

About 5 percent of Iowa is covered by woodlands.

When government official Joseph Street first arrived in Iowa in 1833, he wrote that he had never ridden through a country so full of **game**.

Although the wild turkey is almost extinct in this part of the country, the ring-necked pheasant and the quail remain important game birds.

The Kalsow Prairie Preserve, in Pocahontas County, was created to protect Iowa's wildflowers and prairie grasses.

Blue jays are permanent residents of Iowa.

Iowa is home to a wide variety of animals. The largest wild animal found in the state today is the white-tailed deer. Muskrats, raccoons, coyotes, and foxes also call Iowa home. Other small animals in the state include skunks, groundhogs, rabbits, badgers, minks, and weasels. Many reptiles reside in Iowa, including three species of poisonous snakes—the prairie, the massasauga, and the timber rattlesnakes.

Iowans can look to the skies for more wildlife. Crows, blue jays, cardinals, sparrows, doves, and kingfishers all live in Iowa. Bird-watchers can also spot migrating birds flying south for the winter or north for the summer. Iowa lies along the path of the Mississippi Flyway, which is a north-south migratory route used by millions of birds. Mallards, Canada geese, blue-winged teals, and redheads are among the birds that fly through Iowa.

QUICK FACTS

Many animal species in Iowa, such as the prairie chicken and the passenger pigeon, have become extinct.

Iowa once had large numbers of bison and elk. They have now disappeared from the state.

Iowa's waters are full of smallmouth bass, trout, pike, and carp.

Muskrats and raccoons are still trapped for fur, just as they have been for hundreds of years.

Muskrat

Iowa is home to two types of foxes—the red fox and the gray fox.

The Lewis and Clark State Park is home to a full-sized replica of the keelboat that took Lewis and Clark down the Missouri River.

TOURISM

Iowa's natural beauty is on display to travelers of the Inkpaduta Canoe Trail. The 133-mile trail winds its way down the Little Sioux River and has more than twenty-six designated stops. Those interested in history can follow Meriwether Lewis and William Clark's journey along the Missouri River in the northwest. Across the state, tourists can stop off at Old Fort Madison, situated on the Mississippi River. At the fort, historic interpreters take visitors on a tour of Iowa's rugged frontier heritage.

The Grotto of Redemption at West Bend is the largest **grotto** in the world—it covers one entire city block. The grotto, started by Father Paul Dobbersein, was created by placing gems and colored rocks into concrete. It has been valued at more than $4.3 million and is visited by more than 100,000 people every year.

The popularity of the 1992 novel *The Bridges of Madison County* turned Madison County into a booming tourist destination. While the county was once home to nineteen bridges, today only six remain.

The bridges in Madison County were covered to protect the large floor timbers, which are expensive to replace.

In recent years, Iowa's annual income from farming has been more than $11 billion.

QUICK FACTS

The Duesenberg, a luxury automobile of the early twentieth century, was invented and built by Fred Duesenberg, a Des Moines bicycle shopkeeper.

In 1937, John Vincent Atanasoff and Clifford Berry developed the world's first electronic digital computer at Iowa State University.

Large campers and motor homes known as Winnebagos are named after Winnebago County.

INDUSTRY

Industry in Iowa is closely linked to the needs of the farming sector. The earliest industries were based on mills used to grind wheat into flour. When the price of wheat dropped at the end of the American Civil War, farmers turned to growing corn and to raising hogs and cattle. As a result, pork-packing plants developed, and creameries sprung up to process cow's milk into butter.

Today, Iowa has a strong manufacturing industry. In fact, manufacturing accounts for a greater percentage of Iowa's income than farming. Much of the manufacturing in Iowa is still directly related to agriculture, in the form of food processing and the manufacturing of farm machinery.

Other products manufactured in Iowa include refrigeration equipment, electronic materials, motor homes, rolled aluminum, writing instruments, and small appliances.

The headquarters for Winnebago Industries Inc. is in Forest City. It is the largest motor-home manufacturing facility in the world.

Iowa produces more corn than any other state. More than 1.7 billion bushels of corn are produced every year.

GOODS AND SERVICES

Iowa ranks first among all the states in the production of beef, pork, corn, soybeans, and grains. More than half of the state's corn is used to feed livestock. Some corn is used to make popcorn, breakfast cereal, and other foods. Iowa's corn is also used to make **ethanol**. The state produces nearly 400 million gallons of ethanol per year. Iowan corn is a hybrid corn. This hardy corn is better suited to survive disease and **drought**. Many other midwestern states use Iowa's corn seed to help produce higher-quality crops.

Soybeans also give Iowan farmers a great **yield**. This crop is used to make food products, livestock feed, and industrial goods. Hays, including alfalfa, red clover, and timothy, also grow well throughout the state.

In the 1890s, an Iowan farmer named Jesse Hiatt was the first person to grow red delicious apples on his farm near Peru, Iowa. Today, the red delicious is one of the most popular types of apple in the world.

QUICK FACTS

Every year more than 150 million bushels of Iowa's corn are used in the production of ethanol.

Iowa produces one-tenth of the nation's food supply.

One-quarter of Iowa's exported farm products feed people overseas.

Wheat, vegetables, and apples are all grown in Iowa.

About 25 percent of all hogs sold in the United States come from Iowa.

Iowa is the third-largest livestock producer in the country. Livestock are fattened up on corn and fetch high prices at the markets. Cows are also used for their milk, making Iowa one of the leading states for milk production. Most of the milk is made into butter and cream. Only a small amount is sold fresh. Other farmers raise poultry and make their living from the sale of turkeys, chickens, and eggs.

Government agencies, such as Iowa's Department of Economic Development, sponsor trade missions to encourage economic growth and to maintain the state's successful economy. Agriculture is assisted by the research at Iowa's universities and colleges. Schools like Iowa State University of Science and Technology offer studies in agriculture and veterinary medicine.

The sale of livestock and livestock products contributes about $4.8 billion to Iowa's economy per year.

FIRST NATIONS

The Meskwaki, also known as the Fox, have lived in Iowa since the 1730s.

QUICK FACTS

Many different Native-American groups have lived in Iowa. These include the Omaha, Missouri, Dakota, Winnebago, and Illinois.

Native Americans gave up their last official claim to land in Iowa in 1851.

In 1857, some Meskwaki returned to Iowa and purchased 80 acres of land in what became Tama County.

Fort Atkinson was the only fort ever built by the United States government to protect one Native-American group from another. The fort offered protection to the Winnebago from the Sauk and the Meskwaki.

The first people believed to have lived in Iowa were the Mound Builders. They lived in the area between 2,500 and 10,000 years ago. The Mound Builders left huge dirt mounds that they used for burial ceremonies and for defense. They also left behind evidence of stone carvings, pottery, weaving, and trade systems.

One of the Native-American groups that once lived in the area gave their name to the state of Iowa. The Iowas combined hunting with the agricultural techniques of neighboring Native-American groups. They grew **maize** and lived most of the year in permanent earthen houses. When they hunted, they lived in tepees. The Iowas spoke a language that was related to the Sioux language. They traded furs and clay pipes with the French.

The Iowas surrendered to the United States after a series of conflicts. In 1836, they left their land to the newly arrived settlers. The Iowas once numbered 1,100 in the mid-eighteenth century, but by the late-twentieth century, there were only about 100 Iowas living on a reservation in northeastern Kansas and 100 more in Oklahoma.

The name Meskwaki means "red earth people." The Meskwaki traditionally farmed corn, beans, and squash, and hunted deer for meat.

The Sergeant Floyd Monument in Sioux City is named for the only man who died on the Lewis and Clark expedition.

EXPLORERS AND MISSIONARIES

Father Jacques Marquette and Louis Jolliet were the first Europeans to arrive in Iowa. Jacques Marquette was a Catholic missionary born in France. In 1672, he became **chaplain** for an **expedition** headed by Louis Jolliet. Jolliet was a fur trader who had explored and charted much of the area around the Great Lakes. The goal of the expedition was to explore the areas now known as Minnesota, Iowa, and Illinois. Joined by five other explorers, Marquette and Jolliet crossed Lake Michigan, and the Fox and Wisconsin Rivers. Then they followed the Mississippi River south to Iowa and beyond, before returning home. Louis Jolliet continued to explore and chart many areas of North America until his death in 1700.

In 1681 and 1682, another French expedition explored the area. René-Robert Cavelier, Sieur de La Salle, claimed the entire Mississippi River basin for France. This region, which included Iowa, was named Louisiana.

QUICK FACTS

On his way home from exploring the Mississippi River, Louis Jolliet lost all of his important maps and journals in a canoeing accident. When he returned home, Jolliet reproduced a large part of the information from memory.

Father Marquette remained a missionary in the Lake Michigan area until he died in 1675.

Around 1804, Lewis and Clark crossed Iowa during their exploration of the Louisiana Territory. It was near Sioux City that Sergeant Floyd died of a ruptured appendix.

Father Marquette was one of the first Europeans to explore the Mississippi River.

EARLY SETTLERS

Julian Dubuque was Iowa's first settler of European heritage. He arrived near what is now the city of Dubuque in 1788. After receiving permission from the Meskwaki, Dubuque started a lead-mining operation. Dubuque hired the Meskwaki to work in the mines and then sold the lead in St. Louis. After his death, the Meskwaki took over the company.

In the 1830s, settlers began arriving in the area in large numbers from the eastern states. In 1832, a treaty was signed between the Sauk and the United States government. It made European settlement legal in Iowa. Before 1832, there were fewer than 100 settlers in Iowa, but by 1840 that number had jumped up to 43,000. After Iowa became a state in 1846, the population began to grow again. By 1850, the state was home to more than 190,000 people, many of them European immigrants. Germans were the largest ethnic group, followed by the Irish.

Ambrose Harlan was one of the many pioneers who moved to Iowa to farm the fertile soil.

QUICK FACTS

In 1808, Fort Madison was built along the Mississippi River. The Sauk and the Meskwaki did not enjoy having a United States military fort on their land. The two groups joined the British during the War of 1812 and attacked the fort, burning it to the ground.

Iowa farmers planted rows of trees next to their houses to form a windbreak and give them shade from the hot sun.

Early settlers were once able to grow 200 bushels of corn per acre almost anywhere in the state. Today, that number has dropped to about 150 bushels per acre.

Between 1870 and 1895, about 20,000 people left Denmark to come to the United States. Many of these immigrants settled in Iowa.

In 1835, when the United States Army sent soldiers to scout the Iowa area, the grass on the prairies was so high they could wrap it over their horses' backs and tie it in knots. The wild strawberries were so dense that they stained the horses' hooves red.

Plowing the baked earth for the first time was back-breaking work for the early settlers. The roots of the prairie grasses were extremely thick and sounded like pistol shots when they were torn from the ground. Many farmers believed that the ground released a gas, which gave them and their families a **malarial** fever.

The early settlers farmed on 160-acre sections of land that were divided into quarters. The quarter sections formed an evenly divided grid of farms and small towns across the entire state. Most of the roads in the state run north to south or east to west as a result of this land organization.

QUICK FACTS

Iowa's first library was established in 1853 in Fairfield.

In 1838, Democrat Robert Lucas became the first governor of the Iowa Territory. Burlington was the first capital of the territory. The capital was later moved to Iowa City in 1839 and then to Des Moines in 1857.

Immigrants who fled revolutions and famines in Europe came to Iowa in search of cheap farmland to settle. These pioneers often arrived in Iowa by oxcart.

POPULATION

More than 2.9 million people live in Iowa.

The twentieth century saw Iowa's population change from a mainly rural to a mainly **urban** population. Many people moved to the cities when farmers began replacing workers with machines. In the 1930s, about 60 percent of Iowa's population lived in rural areas. By 1990, less than 40 percent of the population still lived in rural areas. Despite these changes, Iowa's rural population is higher than the national average. By comparison, only 25 percent of the United States population lives in rural areas. Iowa's overall population suffered a decline in the 1980s, as many people left Iowa to look for jobs elsewhere.

Iowa is the thirtieth most-populated state in the country, and has a **population density** of 51 people per square mile. The population density for the United States is 77 people per square mile. People of European heritage make up about 93 percent of the population. The second-largest group is Hispanic American at 2.8 percent, followed by African American at 2.1 percent, Asian at 1.3 percent, and Native American at 0.3 percent.

Cedar Rapids was named for the rapids on the Cedar River. Today, more than 114,500 people call Cedar Rapids home.

QUICK FACTS

Iowa's eight largest cities all boast populations of more than 50,000 people. These cities include Des Moines, Cedar Rapids, Davenport, and Sioux City.

A few hundred Sauk and Meskwaki live on a reservation near Tama. Many others live in cities, including Sioux City.

For the past twenty years, students from Iowa have led the nation in Scholastic Aptitude Test (SAT) scores and American College Test (ACT) scores.

The Capitol, in Des Moines, was completed in 1886.

POLITICS AND GOVERNMENT

Iowa's government is based on a constitution. Like the United States Constitution, it divides the government into executive, legislative, and judicial branches. The executive branch enforces the laws of the state and includes the governor and other executives. The legislative branch is divided into a 100-member House of Representatives and a 50-member Senate. Together they form the General Assembly, which creates Iowa's laws. The judicial branch governs the court system. Nine judges rule on cases in the state's Supreme Court. Judges interpret the laws created by the General Assembly.

Iowa has elected mainly Republican candidates to office since the state's early days. From 1848 to 1968, Iowa sent only seven Democrats to the United States Senate, and the first Democrat governor of Iowa was not elected until the 1930s.

Des Moines is both the capital of Iowa and the state's largest city. The city is home to more than 191,000 people.

The Amana Colonies was one of the longest-lasting communal societies in the world.

CULTURAL GROUPS

In the second half of the nineteenth century and the early part of the twentieth century, many immigrants came to Iowa. These included Germans, Irish, English, Scandinavians, Croatians, Italians, Dutch, Czechs, and African Americans. In the twentieth century, African Americans from the south migrated to the northern and midwestern industrial states in search of work. Many settled in Iowa's larger cities, such as Des Moines and Waterloo.

The Amana Colonies in the eastern part of Iowa was founded by a religious German community. Members of the colony migrated from Buffalo, New York, in 1855. The colony was originally one of the many experiments in **communal** living of the mid-1800s. In 1932, the Amana Society voted to end their communal lifestyle in order to adapt to the modern world. The Amana Church Society was created to maintain the group's religious beliefs.

Since 1935, residents of Pella celebrate their Dutch heritage yearly with flowers, parades, and dances.

QUICK FACTS

Nordic Fest is a three-day celebration of Decorah's Scandinavian community.

The Dutch community of Pella hosts an annual tulip festival.

Elk Horn is the largest rural Danish community in the United States.

The horse and buggy is the main form of transportation for the Amish.

The Amish live near Iowa City and Independence. Amish beliefs often conflict with modern technological practices. Their religious and social traditions include living simple lives without automobiles, electricity, telephones, or other modern **conveniences**. The Amish live in isolated communities and speak a unique **dialect** of German. The Amish are pacifists, which means that they do not believe in violence.

Lamoni, in southern Iowa, is home to a **Mormon** community. It was founded when the Mormons passed through Iowa on their way to Utah to escape **persecution** in New York and Illinois. Some members settled in the area and established a community.

Iowa is also home to Quakers, members of a religious group that helped settle the United States. The Quakers of the Springdale-West Branch area assisted with the Underground Railroad, which helped slaves escape the South before the American Civil War.

President Herbert Hoover's parents were Quakers from West Branch. Their home still stands and is open to visitors.

Grant Wood used his sister, Nan, and his dentist, Dr. B. H. McKeeby, as the models for his well-known painting *American Gothic*.

ARTS AND ENTERTAINMENT

Grant Wood is Iowa's best-known artist. He painted local subjects in a realistic manner. Born in 1892, near Anamosa, Wood was one of the leaders of the regionalist art movement. Regionalist painters were known for their paintings of everyday rural life. Wood's painting *American Gothic* is often considered the most recognizable painting from the United States. Wood remained loyal to Iowa throughout his life. He taught art in the public schools of Cedar Rapids until 1924.

Iowa's numerous colleges and universities are cultural centers that attract symphonies, dance companies, and musical shows from around the world. Iowa showed its commitment to the arts by establishing the first creative writing degree in the United States. The Iowa Writers' Workshop got its start at the University of Iowa during the early part of the twentieth century. This creative writing program has since been copied by universities across North America.

QUICK FACTS

Leon "Bix" Beiderbecke was one of the great jazz musicians of the 1920s. He was born in Davenport in 1903.

In 1991, riverboat gambling was legalized in Iowa for the first time in any state.

Glenn Miller, a trombonist and big-band leader of the 1930s and early 1940s, was born in Clarinda.

The Cedar Rapids Symphony Orchestra held its first concert on April 13, 1923. At the time, the orchestra consisted of forty-eight volunteer musicians.

The Lansing family farm, in Dyersville, was the location for the movie *Field of Dreams*. Visitors to the site are allowed to play ball on the baseball diamond used in the film.

Many well-known actors have come from Iowa. These include Cloris Leachman, William Frawley, Kate Mulgrew, and Harriet Nelson. John Wayne, a popular and rugged movie star, was best known for his roles in Hollywood western films. He was born Marion Robert Morrison in Winterset in 1907. Wayne starred in such films as *True Grit* and *The Searchers*. Soon after his death in 1979, Wayne was awarded the highest civilian honor, the Congressional Gold Medal.

Iowa has also produced a number of talented writers. Wallace Stegner, Abigail van Buren, Susan Glaspell, Elsa Maxwell, David Rabe, and MacKinlay Kantor came from the state. Advice columnist Ann Landers is from Sioux City. Landers is one of the most popular columnists in North America.

John Wayne was an actor in many western films. His characters were patriotic, tough, and heroic cowboys.

The University of Iowa's basketball team has played more than 2,180 games since they first started playing in 1902.

SPORTS

Sporting events are extremely popular in Iowa. The University of Iowa's sports teams, called the Hawkeyes, draw large crowds. Iowans attend the Hawkeyes' football and basketball games in greater numbers than are found at almost any other major university in the country. The Hawkeyes are not just athletes—they also excel in class. Students who participate in athletics at the University of Iowa have a higher graduation rate than any other athletes in the country. They even have a higher graduation rate than their fellow students at the University of Iowa.

The sixty-four other universities and public and private colleges in Iowa also have their own popular athletic programs. High school basketball and wrestling are supported in the winter months across the state.

QUICK FACTS

The University of Northern Iowa recently received a donation to build a new 6,000-seat sports arena, the MacleodUSA Center.

The University of Northern Iowa competes in football, baseball, men's and women's basketball, swimming and diving, and track and field.

In 1999, thirteen Iowa Hawkeye football players earned All-Big Ten academic honors. The All-Big Ten awards are given to top athletes from universities in the Midwest.

Over the past two decades, the Iowa Hawkeyes have won three All-Big Ten Conference titles. They have also had fourteen first division finishes.

QUICK FACTS

The Iowa State Cyclones received their name in 1895, when the football team defeated the better-ranked Northwestern team. This happened only months after major tornadoes had devastated many Iowa farms and towns.

Glenn S. "Pop" Warner, the inventor of the double wingback offense, coached the Iowa Agricultural College (later Iowa State University) football team in its earliest years, during the 1890s.

Fastball pitcher Bob Feller played with the Cleveland Indians from the mid-1930s to the early 1950s. He was from Van Meter and was inducted into the Baseball Hall of Fame in 1962.

The Drake University Bulldogs regularly finish in the upper division of the Missouri Valley Conference in a variety of sports, including football, men's and women's basketball, men's and women's indoor and outdoor track events, soccer, baseball, softball, and volleyball. In the 1999–2000 season, the Bulldogs placed fifth in the Missouri Valley Conference All-Sports standings for men and women. This was higher than any other private university competing that season.

For more than 100 years, the Iowa Great Lakes Region has been a popular vacation spot for water lovers.

Iowans participate in outdoor sports such as hunting, fishing, boating, and camping. More than 100 state parks and recreation areas provide residents with places to hike, cycle, and enjoy water sports.

The Register's Annual Great Bicycle Ride Across Iowa covers 470 miles and lasts seven days.

Brain Teasers

1 Which well-known cereal company got its start in Cedar Rapids?

Answer: Quaker Oats. It is the largest cereal company in the world.

2 In which "lake" can you find the largest bullhead fish in the world?

Answer: The town of Crystal Lake is home to the world's largest statue of a bullhead fish.

3 What is Strawberry Point known for?

Answer: Strawberry Point is the site of the world's largest strawberry. The strawberry was built on top of the city hall.

4 Of all the bridges in Madison County, which one is the longest?

Answer: The Holliwell Bridge is the longest bridge in Madison County. The bridge spans 110 feet and is listed on the National Register of Historic Places.

5

In which year was Iowa's first school opened?

Answer: 1830. The first school was built by Isaac Galland in Lee county.

6

Which United States president was born in Iowa?

Answer: Herbert Hoover was from West Branch. Hoover went on to become the thirty-first president of the United States.

7

One of the first train robberies in the West was committed against the Rock Island train near Adair. Who committed the robbery?

Answer: Frank and Jesse James. The James brothers were joined by outlaws Jim and Cole Younger, Robert Moore, Comanche Tony, and Cell Miller.

8

Which Iowa college campus is also a historic site?

Answer: Cornell College, in Mount Vernon, is the only school in the country whose entire campus is listed on the National Register of Historic Places.

FOR MORE INFORMATION

Books

Richard, Lord Acton. *A Brit Among the Hawkeyes*. Ames: Iowa State University Press, 1998.

Carpenter, Allen. *Between Two Rivers: Iowa Year by Year, 1846–1996*. Ames: Iowa State University Press, 1997.

Dinsmore, James J. *A Country So Full of Game: The Story of Wildlife in Iowa*. Iowa City: University of Iowa Press, 1994.

Reschly, Stephen D. *The Amish of the Iowa Prairie, 1840 to 1910*. Baltimore: John Hopkins University Press, 2000.

Web sites

You can also go online and have a look at the following Web sites:

State of Iowa
http://www.state.ia.us

50 States: Iowa
http://www.50states.com/iowa.htm

The Official Iowa Tourism Home Page
http://www.traveliowa.com

Iowa Counties
http://www.iowa-counties.com

Some Web sites stay current longer than others. To find other Iowa Web sites, enter search terms such as "Iowa," "Des Moines," "Madison County," or any other topic you want to research.

GLOSSARY

Black Hawk War: a conflict fought between Black Hawk and the United States government over land

chaplain: a member of the clergy attached to a private institution or group

communal: a type of lifestyle where all items and possessions are shared within a community

conveniences: modern tools and appliances used to make work easier

dialect: a particular variety of a language, usually specific to a geographic area

drought: a long period of time where there is little or no rain

ethanol: a form of alcohol that can be used as a fuel in automobiles

expedition: a journey made for discovery

game: wild animals hunted for food or sport

grass roots: community or local

grotto: an artificial cave or cavern

gypsum: a mineral made of calcium sulfate

hybrid: a combination of two different plants or animals

Louisiana Purchase: a large amount of territory purchased from France by the United States in 1803

maize: a type of corn

malarial: a disease that causes chills and fevers, carried by mosquitoes

Mormon: a member of the Church of Jesus Christ of Latter-day Saints

persecution: the act of being attacked for one's beliefs

population density: the average number of people per unit of area

precipitation: rain, hail, or snow that falls to the ground

renewable: a resource that can be used over and over, without ever being depleted

rural: relating to the country or countryside, as opposed to the city

urban: relating to the city

watershed: a line of separation between waters flowing to different river basins

windbreaks: trees or bushes that provide shelter from the wind

yield: the amount of a crop produced by cultivation

INDEX

Amana Colonies 7, 22
American Civil War 12,
    13, 23
Amish 23

Black Hawk War 6, 31

Cavelier, René-Robert 17
Cornell College 29

Des Moines 5, 13, 15, 19,
    20, 21, 22
Dubuque (city) 18
Dubuque, Julian 18

Grotto of Redemption 12

Hoover, Herbert 23, 29

Inkpaduta Canoe Trail 12

Jolliet, Louis 17

Landers, Ann 25
Lewis and Clark 12, 17

Madison County 7, 12, 25,
    28
Marquette, Father 17
Miller, Glenn 24
Mississippi River 4, 5, 6,
    8, 17, 18, 23
Missouri River 4, 5, 8, 12
Mormons 23, 31

Native Americans (First
    Nations) 6, 16, 18, 20

Quaker Oats 28
Quakers 23

Reed, Donna 25
Republican Party 7, 21

Sioux City 15, 17, 20, 25

University of Iowa 23, 24,
    26

Wayne, John 25
Winnebago County 13
Wood, Grant 24